AF269452

GREECE

R.L. Van

Big Buddy Books
An Imprint of Abdo Publishing
abdobooks.com

abdobooks.com

Published by Abdo Publishing, a division of ABDO, PO Box 398166, Minneapolis, Minnesota 55439.
Copyright © 2023 by Abdo Consulting Group, Inc. International copyrights reserved in all countries. No part of this book may be reproduced in any form without written permission from the publisher. Big Buddy Books™ is a trademark and logo of Abdo Publishing.

Printed in the United States of America, North Mankato, Minnesota
102022
012023

THIS BOOK CONTAINS RECYCLED MATERIALS

Design: Emily O'Malley, Mighty Media, Inc.
Production: Mighty Media, Inc.
Editor: Jessica Rusick
Cover Photograph: Izabela23/Shutterstock Images
Interior Photographs: Alexandros Michailidis/Shutterstock Images, p. 19; Axel Mel/Shutterstock Images, p. 27 (top left); Cristian Mircea Balate/Shutterstock Images, p. 15; Filip Bjorkman/Shutterstock Images, p. 7 (map); Georgios Tsichlis/Shutterstock Images, pp. 13, 17, 27 (bottom); GK1982/Shutterstock Images, p. 28 (bottom); Izabela23/Shutterstock Images, p. 25; Juassawa/Shutterstock Images, p. 30 (flag); Larina Marina/Shutterstock Images, p. 6 (bottom); Lucian BOLCA/Shutterstock Images, p. 26 (right); Lucky-photographer/Shutterstock Images, p. 27 (top right); lukulo/iStockphoto, pp. 5 (compass), 7 (compass); Martin Baldwin-Edwards/Flickr, p. 29 (bottom); Maryna Pleshkun/Shutterstock Images, p. 30 (currency); Pyty/Shutterstock Images, p. 5 (map); Richard Whitcombe/Shutterstock Images, p. 9; S.Dali/Shutterstock Images, p. 28 (top); Sven Hansche/Shutterstock Images, p. 6 (top); trabantos/Shutterstock Images, p. 6 (middle); Truba7113/Shutterstock Images, p. 29 (top); Ververidis Vasilis/Shutterstock Images, p. 23; Wikimedia Commons, pp. 11, 21; Zaharia Bogdan Rares/Shutterstock Images, p. 26 (left)
Design Elements: Mighty Media, Inc.
Country population and area figures taken from the CIA World Factbook

Library of Congress Control Number: 2022940509

Publisher's Cataloging-in-Publication Data
Names: Van, R.L., author.
Title: Greece / by R.L. Van
Description: Minneapolis, Minnesota : Abdo Publishing, 2023 | Series: Countries | Includes online resources and index.
Identifiers: ISBN 9781532199622 (lib. bdg.) | ISBN 9781098274825 (ebook)
Subjects: LCSH: Greece--Juvenile literature. | Europe--Juvenile literature. | Greece--History--Juvenile literature. | Geography--Juvenile literature.
Classification: DDC 949.5--dc23

CONTENTS

PASSPORT TO GREECE

Greece is a country in southern Europe. It is bordered by three seas and four countries. About 10.5 million people live there.

DID YOU KNOW?

The dolphin is Greece's national animal.

WHERE IS GREECE?
N
W E
S
Bulgaria
Macedonia
Albania
GREECE
Aegean Sea
Turkey
Ionian Sea
Mediterranean Sea

IMPORTANT CITIES

Athens is Greece's **capital** and largest city. It is known for its history, education, and arts.

Thessaloniki is Greece's second-largest city. It is a large port city known for its culture, food, and nightlife.

Patras is Greece's third-largest city. Its busy port connects Greece to Italy. Patras is known for its education and Carnival.

SAY IT

Athens
ATH-enz

Thessaloniki
THEH-sah-loh-NEE-kee

Patras
PAT-truss

DID YOU KNOW?

Athens is considered to be where Western **civilization** began.

GREECE IN HISTORY

People have lived in Greece for thousands of years. The first known **civilization** was the Minoan civilization. The Mycenaean civilization controlled Greece between 1700 and 1100 BCE.

SAY IT

Minoan
muh-NOH-uhn

Mycenaean
mye-suh-NEE-uhn

Minoan ruins are preserved on the island of Crete.

Beginning around 700 BCE, Greeks lived in city-states. These areas had their own governments. Around 507 BCE, Athens became the world's first known democracy.

The Ottoman **Empire** took power in the 1400s. Greece began a war for independence in 1821. It was fully independent by 1832.

British, French, and Russian forces helped the Greeks win naval battles during the war for independence.

AN IMPORTANT SYMBOL

Greece's flag is white and blue. Its cross is for the Greek Orthodox faith. The stripes stand for independence.

Greece is a **parliamentary republic**. The Hellenic Parliament makes laws. The prime minister is head of government. The president is head of state.

To Greeks, blue represents the sea and sky. White represents waves and clouds.

ACROSS THE LAND

Greece has the longest coastline in Europe. It also has mountains, forests, lakes, and **volcanoes**.

Greece has deer, wild boars, and many types of birds. Olive, cypress, and fir trees grow there. Oranges, lemons, and grapes do too.

The Greek island of Corfu has dozens of beaches.

EARNING A LIVING

Most Greek people have service jobs, such as working for the government. Greek factory workers make cloth and food products.

Greece's **natural resources** include **bauxite** and marble. Seafood comes from its waters. Farmers grow corn, wheat, olives, and fruits.

Three-quarters of Greece's olives are grown on the island of Crete.

LIFE IN GREECE

Most Greeks live in cities. Others live on islands or in rural areas. Favorite Greek foods include olive oil, lamb, and feta cheese. Coffee is a popular drink.

Soccer and basketball are popular in Greece. Most Greeks are members of the Greek Orthodox Church.

Greeks dance to celebrate at a festival on the island of Serifos.

FAMOUS FACES

Maria Callas was a world-famous opera singer. She was born in New York to Greek parents in 1923. In 1937, Callas returned to Greece. She studied music there. Callas first sang at the Athens Opera at age 17. She went on to sing all over the world.

Callas performs at a concert in Amsterdam, Netherlands, in July 1959.

Giannis Antetokounmpo was born in Athens to Nigerian parents. He was drafted by the **National Basketball Association's (NBA)** Milwaukee Bucks in 2013 at age 18. In 2021, he helped the Bucks win their first NBA championship in 50 years. He also plays for the Greek national team.

Giannis Antetokounmpo won the NBA's Most Valuable Player award in 2019 and 2020.

A GREAT COUNTRY

Greece is known for its beautiful land and long history. The people and places of Greece help make the world a more interesting place.

Villages along the Greek coast often have colorful homes and buildings.

TOUR BOOK

If you ever visit Greece, here are some places to go and things to do!

EXPLORE

Hike up Mount Olympus, Greece's tallest peak.

DISCOVER

Visit Santorini to wander cobblestone streets and swim at **volcanic** beaches that can have black or red sand.

EAT

Try custard-filled *bougatsa* at a bakery in Thessaloniki.

LEARN

Visit the Parthenon, a 2,000-year-old temple. Learn about the ancient site at the nearby Acropolis Museum.

PLAY

Swim, snorkel, and more on Elafonisi Beach in Crete.

TIMELINE

ABOUT 460 BCE

Hippocrates was born. His ideas changed the practice of medicine.

1821 CE

The Greek War of Independence began.

447-438 BCE

The Parthenon was built. It became one of Greece's most famous buildings.

336 BCE

Alexander the Great became king of the Greek kingdom of Macedon. He spread Greek culture across his **empire**.

2009

A serious **economic** crisis began in Greece. The country is still recovering today.

2020

Katerina Sakellaropoulou was elected Greece's first female president.

1896

The first modern Olympics were held in Athens. Ancient Greeks had held Olympic Games for hundreds of years.

GREECE
UP CLOSE

Official Name
Elliniki Dimokratia
(Hellenic Republic)

Flag

Population
10,533,871 (2022 est.)
88th-most-populated country

Total Area
50,949 square miles
(131,957 sq km)
96th-largest country

Official Language
Greek

Capital
Athens

Currency
Euro

Form of Government
Parliamentary republic

National Anthem
"Ymnos eis tin
Eleftherian"
("Hymn to Liberty")

GLOSSARY

bauxite (BAWK-site)—a substance that is the main source of aluminum. Aluminum is a silver-colored, lightweight metal. It is used in making machinery and other products.

capital—a city where government leaders meet.

civilization—a well-organized and advanced society.

economic—having to do with a society's ways of making, distributing, and using goods and services.

empire—a large group of states or countries under one ruler called an emperor or empress.

National Basketball Association (NBA)—a North American professional basketball league.

natural resources—useful and valuable supplies from nature.

parliamentary republic—a government that has a leader who is usually a president, not a king or queen, and a parliament that makes laws.

volcano—a deep opening in Earth's surface from which hot liquid rock or steam comes out. Something related to a volcano is volcanic.

ONLINE RESOURCES

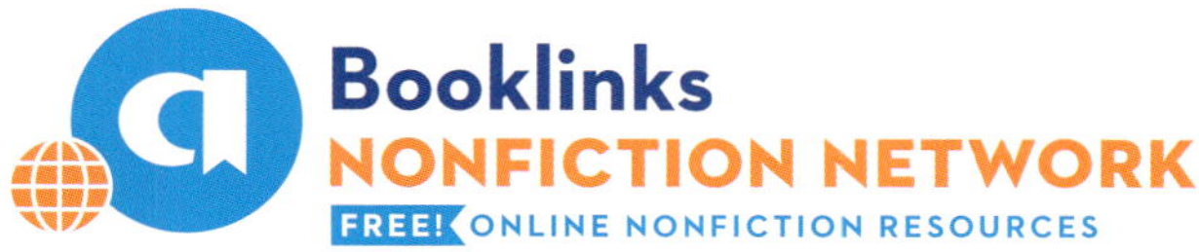

To learn more about Greece, please visit **abdobooklinks.com** or scan this QR code. These links are routinely monitored and updated to provide the most current information available.

INDEX